Also by Kay Bain Weiner:

Stained Glass Magic Book
Solder Magic Video Tape
Solder Magic Book

Line and Color Magic For Glass Design

by

Kay Bain Weiner

Published by Eastman

First Edition
Published in the United States By Eastman

ISBN 0-9625663-1-4

Distributed by: Canfield Quality Solder
                  Post Office Box 3100
                  Union, New Jersey 07083

"Gratitude is the least articulate of the emotions, especially when it is deep."

Felix Frankfurter

DEDICATION

This book is dedicated to all my wonderful students who have inspired me to write it.

My deepest appreciation goes to my huband, Herb, for his encouragement and assistance.

ACKNOWLEDGMENTS

My sincere gratitude to the special people whose combined talents and enthusiasm helped shape this book and bring it to fruition. Many thanks: Martha Sides, Leona and Boris Levine, Allan Warner.

CREDITS

Walter Paist for expertise in photography.
Julius Benevento for the cover art.

Sketches, illustrations, and glass art by the author unless otherwise noted.

PERMISSION

Muriel Caffee of Camur Design Products: patterns.

Charleen Swansea: reprint from her book, *Mindworks*, © 1990 by South Carolina ETV and Charleen Swansea.

Workshop students: Leona Griner, Dorothy Jiles Hamilton, James R. Johnson, Barbara Parish, Robert Vellum, Martha Williamson for examples of designing exercises.

Color Wheel reprinted by permission of M. Grumbacher, Inc. © 1972. All rights reserved.

Illustrations and photos reproduced from *Composition* by J. M. Parramon published by HP Books, a division of Price Stern Sloan, Inc., Los Angeles, California. © 1981 by Fisher Publishing, Inc.

Illustrations reproduced from *Creative Color* by Faber Birren, Schiffer Publishing Ltd., courtesy of Mrs. Birren.

"Look within yourself for inspiration"

KBW

TABLE OF CONTENTS

Chapter one
MAGICAL ILLUSIONS OF LINE AND COLOR

"The greatness of art is not to find what is common but what is unique."

Isaac Bashevis Singer

A glass artist translates the language of line and color to communicate emotions through images. Creativity is the magical process of originating an innovative idea or revising an existing concept. How can you tap into your own creative resources? How do you obtain this mystical power? Stimulating your inventiveness and sparking the imagination can expand your creative potential.

You can become a more creative thinker and improve your drawing and designing skills. This book will "draw out the artist from within" and allow the magic to emerge to the surface. It will enable you to understand the components that make up the creative personality. Exercises of brainstorming and imagery are techniques that you can use to develop intuitive visualization and more vivid imagination to venture into new areas of exploration.

Through these pages you are invited to participate in a series of exercises and procedures that are designed to develop free-flowing ideas, creative intuition, self-confidence, and a better understanding of the interplay of color and line dynamics.

Numerous illustrations, photos, and examples demonstrate how to use color and design relationships to enhance your glass art. The book discusses the expressive quality of line and using it effectively to convey a mood or suggest depth. Learn how color relationships can create optical illusions or a focal point and how they complement one another.

Gain knowledge about how to use glass colors and textures harmoniously and create an exciting, balanced composition. Several chapters contain practical advice about designing and drawing your own patterns and enlarging designs. Valuable tips are included for selecting glass and displaying finished pieces.

The field of glass art emphasizes excellence in craftsmanship. Most books to date present glass crafting techniques and an array of patterns. However, there is little available which instructs the craftsperson on composition, drawing, and color selection. Much of the information in this text is based on scientific theory and research findings about color, line, and creativity. You will discover surprises in line and color that you can apply to work in any craft medium.

Many craftspersons work in their accustomed style, technique and subject matter, which can become stale and uninspiring. It is time to go beyond your traditional working methods to explore new possibilities. The ideas in this book can augment your present style and give you new perspective which challenges you to reach for greater heights.

It is my sincere hope that this book will become a guide you will refer to again and again. May the information serve as stepping stones to lead you through more creative paths.

"As is our confidence, so is our capacity."

William Hazlitt

Line and Color Magic for Glass Design

Chapter Two
GIFT OF CREATIVITY

"Creativity, contrary to firmly entrenched folklore, is not the province or preserve of only a few talented individuals ..."

Eugene Raudsepp

How can we tap into our own creative resources? Creativity is a magical process. It is the process of originating a new idea through inventing, revising or augmenting an existing entity. Not everyone sees himself or herself as a creative person, thinking, "I have written no compelling novels, painted no timeless murals, built no towering buildings." Yet the act of everyday living is an exercise in creativity. The tie or scarf you choose for a particular occasion, the color of the towels you select to coordinate with the bathroom wallpaper, the flowers you plant around your front door to accent the color of the shutters, are examples of your personal creativity.

Part of the joy of creativity is the elation that comes as ideas fall into place and images take form. There is distinct pleasure in combining unusual textures, discovering a striking color scheme, employing a newly-mastered technique, or developing a theme.

Risky Business

Dr. Joyce Brothers writes that creative people must be willing to take risks which may lead to failure. Risk-ing failure is necessary to test original ideas. Creative people share some common characteristics: they are open to new ideas, display an insatiable curiosity, think in images rather than words, are willing to take chances with their ideas, and are not perfectionists.

The creative person always searches for the innovative and reaches for new perspectives. Attending classes on unfamiliar techniques or expanding your knowledge can open new vistas. Working in a group can be stimulating since it often triggers an electric flow of ideas–an artistic form of brainstorming. There is a give and take and an exchange of information which frequently produces more excitement than working alone. Peer critiquing, which is part of the process, is a valuable aspect of group dynamics.

In order to generate new ideas, you must be willing to discard your inhibitions and insecurities. Try to break habitual stale thought patterns. Be flexible. Discipline yourself to visualize the potential of the ordinary by discovering its uniqueness.

Try new concepts. There is safety in the familiar working patterns with the usual tools, techniques, and styles. Accept change so that you can grow as an artist! Change renews creative energy.

Although it is easier to continue in your accustomed style and color schemes, your working habits and finished product can become boring and predictable. The opportunities are unlimited if you are willing to explore new avenues. Develop confidence in your instincts.

Set aside the time to play and explore. With the pressures of everyday commitments, it is difficult to steal the moments we need to refresh our minds. Try to release the stress of everyday problems that interrupt the flow of creative thoughts. Use this time as a fun learning period to plant the seeds of new ideas. When you are in a relaxed frame of mind, ideas usually flow more freely. When an idea hits you, it may be a grain of a thought that needs time to germinate.

Creating can be spontaneous, and its result is a powerful visual language to express inner and outer emotion. By observing and doing you will become more adept and gain confidence in your ability and judgment. The road to success is achieved by accepting your own level of accomplishment at each stage of your artistic development.

The ability to commit a design to paper is not limited to the trained artist. Many of you are inclined to believe that you cannot design or draw, that you are not "artistic." You must abandon that idea! Start working to become more artistic in all your endeavors.

Technique and the rules of line and design can be learned. But your creativity is the catalyst for sparking a reaction between the components and the finished product. Although there are many theories about color relationships and line design, they must be guided by your intuition and imagination.

A spontaneous sketch was developed into a piece of etched glass art.

Brainstorming

Brainstorming is a technique used for stimulating thought patterns and making connections so that ideas flow abundantly. It is also a valid method of clearing the mind, so that subconscious thought waves might surface freely.

As Charleen Swansea suggests in her book, *Mindworks*, this technique might help you generate ideas and think of fresh subject matter for future projects.

RULES FOR BRAINSTORMING

1. Set an amount of time, like five minutes or 15 minutes.
2. You'll be going fast, so get someone to write down the ideas as they come. Try to get as many ideas as you can in the time limit.
3. Anything goes, so do not judge ideas as good or bad. In fact, the wilder and crazier the ideas seem, the better the brainstorming session will be.
4. Try to hook ideas together. In other words, feel free to build on what another person has said, or connect or expand an idea you already had.
5. Finally, select the best idea.

from Mindworks

Visualization

Your imagination is a marvelous tool if you allow it freedom to lead you down creative paths. Learn to develop a selective eye by storing impressions in the "filebox" of your memory. You may not utilize that fragment of an idea for awhile, but it will rise to the surface if you train your mind to think freely–imaginatively.

So how does this training become second nature to you?

Visualization is one method of training your mind to release creative impulses. A free association of thoughts, visualization is a technique used by many writers, artists, actors to stimulate the thought process. The subconscious is a storehouse of fertile ideas and colorful memories. By clearing the conscious mind of daily thoughts and chores, you can reach and tap into your inner self. It helps the mind project concepts clearly while racing ahead, searching, selecting, and rejecting approaches to the desired goal–whether it be a paragraph, painting, stage scene or glass art project.

To become more creative, allow yourself the freedom, time, and luxury to participate in the almost dream-like activity of visualization. To begin your experiment in this process, set the stage. Dedicate a period of time in a tranquil setting where you will be undisturbed. Use whatever method you find most relaxing until you are free of stress and tension. If it takes a glass of wine, your favorite music, putting your feet up, or meditating– whatever – get ready to use the right side of your brain and begin creative visualization. At the end of this chapter is an exercise which will help you apply this technique.

People who use a visualization method would agree that it is better than a coffee break and more revitalizing than a nap. This process may seem difficult at first, but with practice you will be able to take advantage of your imaging facility. Visualizing is a skill that enables you to imagine and intuitively perceive things with a clearer perspective. This technique can help you become more adept at creative endeavors.

Visualization exercise

Close your eyes. Try to completely relax your body by concentrating on every muscle in your body in turn from your toes to the top of your head. Take several deep breaths, concentrating only on your breathing. When you feel your body relax, visualize yourself walking through a heavily wooded forest. It is summer and the smell of fragrant leaves and wildflowers permeates the air. You hear a small waterfall in the distance, as well as singing birds and rustling animals. You feel the soft moss, small branches, and cool dirt under your bare feet.

The brilliant, golden sunlight streams through the trees, dappling the forest floor. The violet-glossed leaves seem to dance as they sway around the coppery branches. You stop in your thoughts to savor the refreshing breeze. You find a comfortable place to lie down, your body feels very light, and your mind is drifting into space.

It is at this point that your mind is able to capture wandering images and colors and textures. Some of you, at this point, may be tempted to take a nap. However, a more productive use of your relaxed state is to record the ideas that have come to you in this relaxed frame of mind. Use your sketchpad or tape recorder to jot down these ideas. This type of exercise may take practice and variation to be effective for each individual.

"Reverie is the groundwork of creative imagination."

W. Somerset Maugham

Chapter Three
ART AND SOUL

"Any new formula which suddenly emerges in our consciousness has its roots in long trains of thought."
Oliver Wendell Holmes, Sr.

Past experiences and memories are part of the unconscious. They shape your present thoughts, feelings, and viewpoints. Your imagination is interwoven with memory, and it influences intuition and the ability to translate what you see. What inspires one person may not necessarily inspire another. Because you "draw from within," you will probably be more successful at drawing or depicting subjects you are familiar with and enjoy.

You do not duplicate the exact image you see; the drawing or creation is your perception of that image. As an artist you internalize your vision and express feelings about it in your work. It is an artist's license to reinterpret what is seen and alter the reality to suit special needs: an impression of dominant colors, an abstraction, or a realistic translation. The quality of a drawing is based not only on the dexterity of the hand in depicting the image, but also on the accuracy of the visual perception and memory.

Visual awareness and envisioning a composition can be learned and developed intuitively. Become more observant, studying the shapes and colors of everything around you. Allow your eyes to encompass and appreciate your subject matter. Absorb the whole vision and don't try to see every detail. When you look at a tree, notice the flow of branches, the movement of birds and clouds around the tree. Enjoy the moment and try to make really seeing things a part of your life. Not only will this be good training for you as an artist, but it can also enhance your life experiences.

Recent studies suggest that the brain is divided into two halves. The right hemisphere is the creative side; the left is the home of logical thought. The left side is the verbal and rational processor. It is the right side that thinks in the abstract, processes the imaging and visualizing. In her book, *Drawing on the Right Side of the Brain,* author Betty Edwards presents methods to release your creative potential and to tap into the special artistic abilities of the right side of the brain. Drawing techniques can be learned. Most people lack confidence in their own ability to draw, but like most skills, with some practice, your competency can be improved.

Relax your noodle while you doodle

Doodling can be an excellent method of learning to draw, and it comes naturally to most people. As a form of free association it can be very relaxing. Doodling also stimulates the imagination. Sometimes a small, unconscious sketch can be the beginning of an original design–a gift from the artist within. Make a conscious effort to choose a subject. When you have a few free moments while sipping coffee or talking on the telephone, let your hand draw intuitively. If worthy, your doodle can easily be augmented and enlarged to form the basis of your next project. Use tracing paper over your sketch to refine the details of your drawing. It may take two or three tracings until you are satisfied.

Doodling stimulates your imagination while you sketch from your subconscious

Dreams and themes

Where do ideas come from? Frequently they emerge while in a dream state just before falling asleep or immediately upon waking. Many writers and artists take advantage of this fertile period when their thoughts are most prolific. Your sketchbook or doodle pad belongs next to your bed to capture these floating ideas.

Some people prefer to draw or write in a journal daily events or random thoughts, while others have a tape recorder available in order to verbalize impressions.

Ideas submitted to the subconscious for evaluation or solution can be released during visualization or at some special moment, perhaps when least expected. Visualization is detailed in the chapter entitled, "Gift of Creativity."

Keep a sketchbook handy at all times. While away from your studio, you may suddenly be inspired by something you see along the way. When sketching, try to work quickly to record the total concept without concentrating on incidental details. Train yourself to draw ideas and make notes of color and other particulars. Refine the details or enlarge the sketch later if necessary. This spontaneous method of drawing can sometimes be more creatively successful than a painstakingly well-drafted design. Don't be afraid to make a mistake. You can learn from a mistake because it gives you more experience to draw upon. Don't aim for perfection. A perfectionist is never satisfied and sometimes loses the spontaneous surprise and joy of creation.

"Perfection has one grave defect: it is likely to be dull."

W. Somerset Maugham

Advertisements and greeting cards can inspire ideas. Magazine ad on the left; sketch on the right

Although you may have an idea "filebox" in your head, a real filebox is a most helpful tool. Often it is difficult to draw a realistic object such as a chair from memory. A reference file of clippings from magazines, newspapers, greeting cards, labels, and catalogues will help. When you see an advertisement or a color combination which intrigues you, clip and file it. Manila folders can separate animals, people, landscapes, folk art, marine scenes, etc. Further, divide ideas that you could utilize in various mediums, such as fusing, sandblasting, or leading panels. Refer to these files when you need inspiration or incorporate some of these topics in your design.

A camera is an important tool for the artist or craftsperson seeking good subject matter or inspiration. Photographs of subjects might become the basis for projects; sort these into your reference files. Taking photographs also helps you think in terms of composition.

While browsing through my files, I came across a magazine clipping of Spanish dancers. In the free association thought process, I visualized dancers in a chorus line that is now captured in the large, three dimensional fused and stained glass panel which is pictured here.

A newspaper ad prompted me to conceptualize not one but two projects using identical themes, one in stained glass and one in fused glass. The realization that various types of glass could convey the idea of flowing water, the floor, a towel, a shower curtain, etc. prompted great enthusiasm planning the two panels.

Above: The advertisement on the left inspired the fused glass panel on the right. Below: A stained glass panel uses the same theme.

Arts and scraps

Develop your intuitive creative eye. As you browse through your glass scrap bin you will recognize potential projects among the findings. Shapes themselves will suggest designs. Colors lying next to each other might reveal an entirely new color combination. Many glass crafters habitually refer to pattern books rather than relying on their own instincts.

The box lid pictured is an example of random scrap pieces assembled into a free-form design combining metal and glass. Here is an exercise that might help you get your creative motor in gear.

Recycle scraps into a boxtop

Study your glass scraps. Select three or four random pieces that you

can craft into a boxtop. Do not use a pattern, but turn the pieces in all directions until you see a satisfying design. Keep glass cutting down to a minimum and try using the pieces as they are. Keep in mind that a box top does not have to be square or rectangular but can be an odd shape, three-dimensional, or overlaid. You can include globs, jewels, fused glass, sheet copper, and decorative soldering techniques. [The technique for combining metal and glass can be found in the *Solder Magic Book* by Kay Weiner, published by Eastman.]

Study and observe

Avail yourself of every opportunity to visit galleries, museums, craft shops, and shows. A work of art, an artifact, a craft object, or a poster sparks an idea, a clipping from your memory filebox comes to mind, and suddenly a revelation occurs.

As you are exposed to other craft media, you can borrow different techniques. Combining craft media can result in a unique art piece.

To keep your work current and saleable, study new style trends in the furniture and home decorating market. Different color schemes are popular each season, and they are often related to the style that is in vogue. In the Southwestern motif, you will find the influence of Indian design and the natural colors of earth, sky, and sand. These patterns and color relationships can be adapted to stained glass art.

Observe fabric and wallpaper designs. The artists who create these patterns have had years of training, and their sense of color is impeccable. You can cull fresh ideas from their patterns and colors. A floral or abstract pattern could be enlarged and used in a stained glass panel. Find inspiration in the upholstery pattern of your favorite chair or museum poster, greeting card, or needlepoint footstool. You can combine parts or pieces of a motif and create your own "stew," seasoning it with the spice of your own fertile imagination.

"Just as our eyes need light in order to see, our minds need ideas in order to conceive."

Nicolas Malebranche

Chapter Four
IN LIVING COLOR

"Colors and symbols sing to us, and as we hear them, our bodies, psyches and souls respond."

Anne Michael James

Colors and symbols speak to human beings. Art is a visual language that is infused with the energy of the artist. Like music, people respond to art with mind and psyche, which are affected in both positive and negative ways.

Webster defines color as "the sensation resulting from stimulation of the retina of the eye by light waves of certain length." Light comprises all the colors; each color has its own measurable frequency and wave length. The differences in wave lengths are the basis of each color. Sunlight is a combination of all colors of the spectrum, visible and invisible. Because of the differences in the wave lengths and refraction of the rays of each color, the more luminous a color (such as yellow), the closer it appears. Bright and light jump forward.

In 1666, Sir Isaac Newton developed the first valuable theory of color. As illustrated, Newton showed that when a beam of white light passes through a prism, it is refracted and broken up into the colors of the spectrum. He established the presence of seven basic colors: red, orange, yellow, green, blue, indigo, and violet.

The fascination for color has sparked the human imagination since

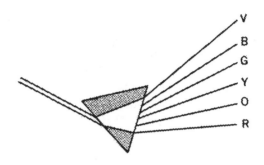

When a beam of light passes through a prism it is reflected and broken up into the colors of the spectrum.

the beginning of time. The scientific study of the subject has proven that color and its energy have a dramatic effect on people's lives, influencing their well-being and state of mind. Health, temperament, comfort, and interaction with others are all influenced by color.

As a glass artist you have the enjoyable, but sometimes confusing, task of selecting harmonious color combinations. Although individual perception and preference of color is personal, artists base color schemes on climate, fashion trend, interior decor, national tradition, and a host of other factors. Color plays magic tricks. By understanding the emotional language of color and the secrets of color theory, you can successfully play matchmaker with colors. Your designs will be enhanced whether your work is contemporary, imaginary, whimsical, or traditional.

Color me emotional

Psychologists suggest that colors evoke emotional responses that have different meanings to different people.

Colors have a compelling effect on each other as well as on the viewer. Generally speaking, hues on the red side of the color spectrum are warm colors and more stimulating, while those on the blue side are cool colors and more sedative. The skill of mixing hot and cool colors can result in a more successful, harmonious visual effect.

Most colors have a positive and a negative association. What images do you perceive when you think of black..? blue..? white..? purple..?

While various cultures and religions interpret color psychology differently, there is a fixed symbolism associated with colors; the mind is subconsciously aware of these images. Used in ancient art, colors had significant symbolic inferences and were carefully chosen. According to psychologists, the box below suggests the images most associated with colors.

Shades of color can also suggest various meanings. Navy or royal blue looks dignified and wealthy while light blue looks young and sporty.

Color contrasts

Certain colors define patterns more clearly than others. By observing advertisements, wrappers, and billboards, you can tell how the professionals use color to their advantage. Color reinforces the image you see, while variation of light and dark value enhances your perception of the image.

You might think that the clearest of

	Positive Associations	Negative Associations
BLACK:	Mighty, dignified, stark, sophisticated	Despair, evil, death
BLUE:	Devotion, truth, cold	Doubt, stormy sea
RED:	Love, life, passion	Danger, devil, war
WHITE:	Purity, peace, wisdom	Ghostly, blank, cold
GRAY:	Mature, humble, discreet	Depression, grief, indifference, barrenness
PURPLE:	Royal, powerful, truthful, patient	Submission, humility, mourning
YELLOW:	Happy, divine, love	Cowardly, mean, deceitful
GREEN:	Tranquility, fertility	Mildew, poison, jealousy
PINK:	Universal, love, healing	

all patterns would be those produced in black and white; however, notice that on the following list, black on white offers less of a contrast than black on yellow. The relative carrying power of different color combinations is listed in order of clarity.

1. **Black on yellow**
2. **Green on white**
3. **Red on white**
4. **Blue on white**
5. **White on blue**
6. **Black on white**
7. **Yellow on black**
8. **White on red**
9. **White on green**
10. **White on black**
11. **Red on yellow**
12. **Green on red**
13. **Red on green**

Color menu

Analogous Colors - tones of the same hue; adjacent or neighboring colors on the color wheel.

Color Wheel - the twelve primary, secondary, and intermediate colors arranged to show how they are related. Several important colors for stained glass artists are missing from the wheel, such as pink, brown, and grey.

Complementary Colors - those hues opposite on the color wheel which,

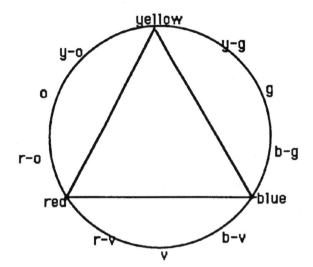

when mixed together, will produce a neutral grey: red/green, yellow/violet, orange/blue.

Hue - a specific color, such as red, orange, yellow; an interchangeable term for color.

Intensity (also **purity, saturation, chroma**) - the degree of departure of a hue from neutral grey. Pure colors have high or strong intensity; tints and shades have low or weak intensity.

Intermediate Colors - all the hues between the primary and secondary colors on the color wheel. They are produced by the mixture of the primary and secondary colors.

Monochromatic Color - one singular

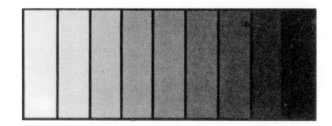

color; monochromatic colors consist of a very small range of wave lengths.

Primary Colors - red, yellow, blue.

Secondary Colors - orange, green, purple.

Tertiary Colors - created when two secondary colors are mixed together, forming a brown hue.

Tint - a color mixed with white.

Tones - variations and graduations that result from the dilution of a hue with white or black. White weakens its tone; black deepens it.

Value, brightness - the lightness or darkness of a hue as compared with the steps of a grey scale. Yellow has a hue of high brightness or value because it is closer to white, and violet has a low value because it is closer to black. Dark colors give the impression of weight; conversely, light colors give a feeling of buoyancy.

The study of color theory is a fascinating pursuit. Becoming more acquainted with the color wheel and some of the basic principles of color relationship can help whether you are a novice or an advanced stained glass artist. Please refer to the color wheel in the color section, chapter 5.

"The purest and most thoughtful minds are those which love colour the most."
John Ruskin

Chapter five
Color Power

"Colors speak all languages."

Joseph Addison

With a little know-how you can become a color magician. Understanding the relationship of color and line enables an artist to use its impact effectively so that the viewer's eye will be captivated. Fascinating linear patterns and color harmonies should be so intriguing that the eye is focused within the framework of the panel.

This chapter will discuss the creation of optical illusions, depth, visual interest, and tricks to give your art pieces more aesthetic pizazz. The information presented here, based on research findings by scientists and psychologists, has been practiced by the most famous artists throughout the ages.

No color performs magic tricks by itself. It needs others to execute its visual wizardry. A color has its hue because of its proximity and relationship to other colors. You must see the total picture of combined hues and values to judge an individual color.

The color selections in Van Gogh's paintings may seem primitive to the untrained eye. However, his work demonstrates that he understood color harmony and the modulation of value painting (using one color from its lightest to its darkest). He brilliantly executed color mixtures–warms and cools, complementary and non-complementary–and breaking of tones with the use of heavy brush strokes of varying shades. Van Gogh used color psychologically to evoke emotions. His painting *Sunflowers*, for example, uses yellow symbolically as pure light and love. In *Starry Night*,

blue symbolizes infinity as in the night sky. Please refer to chapter six.

Analogous color schemes

If your project plans call for an analogous color scheme, do not use more than one-third of these adjacent hues on the color wheel. It is important to vary the value, intensity, and placement of the colors to liven up what could become a boring project. For example, if you are creating an analogous blue and green panel, a touch of orange (the complement of green) could give the picture a vibrant impact.

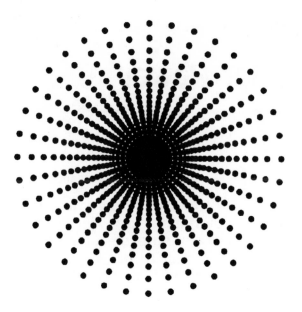

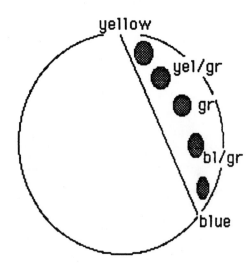

Analogous color scheme

side by side, for example, yellow and purple, each seems more intense than if it were by itself. The strongest opposition of hue is provided by the pure primary colors (red, yellow, and blue).

Complementary color combos

When selecting a complementary color scheme (hues opposite each other on the color wheel) such as blue and orange or violet and yellow, never use them in equal proportions or intensities. Make one hue more dominant and the other less vibrant, or smaller in area, or varied in tone. Weave the warm colors through the cools to create depth and interest. An exception is Op-art, which uses two complements in equal amounts and intensity to create a pulsating sensation. If two complementary colors are

Non-complementary color mysteries

In non-complementary color schemes, the colors relate to one another differently. In the color chart, notice that the large magenta square on the yellow background tends toward purple; whereas the smallest square on the large background intensifies, and its tone tends toward the red-brown. Small colored surfaces placed on an extensive color background will not stand out as strongly when the two colors are non-complementary.

• **Dark hues** on a non-complementary dark ground, such as royal blue on a green background, will appear weaker than on a complementary ground, such as royal blue on red.

• **Light colors** on a non–complementary light ground, such as pale yellow on a white background, will also appear weaker than on a complementary ground, such as pale yellow on lavender.

These weak color combinations can be strengthened greatly if they are bounded by complementary colors.

Experiment I:

Cut two one-inch strips of pale blue construction paper and place each strip on a sheet of light green paper. Cut a two-inch strip of orange paper and place it under one of the blue strips. Stand back. Notice how much brighter the blue appears when it is surrounded by its complement, orange. The blue next to the green paper seems pale and weak.

• Dark hues, such as purple, red, etc., appear stronger if surrounded by light complementary colors or narrow bands of white.

• Light colors, such as yellow or pale green, appear stronger if surrounded by dark complementary colors or narrow

Illusion of depth is created because of value changes, the black appears to be a hole.

bands of black. See color chart.

Colors are influenced in hue by adjacent color, each tinting its neighbor with the complement.

Experiment II:

Take two pieces of colored paper, one yellow and one blue. Cut two equal circles of green or, for convenience, use stick-on colored discs available at stationery and art supply stores.

Place each circle in the center of the colored sheets. Note that the green against the yellow looks both smaller and darker in value. The green against the blue takes on a yellow cast and looks larger. For instance, if you were working with other colors, blue in contrast would appear purplish.

Create depth

Understanding how warm and cool colors work together helps you create spatial relationships within your design. Warm oranges and reds can be bright in the foreground. However, to create an illusion of depth when using them in the distance or background, select reds or yellows that are less intense. Using the same intense colors throughout a panel would make it appear flat and uninteresting. Used in the background, intense colors "jump out of the picture," so you should tone them down.

If dark glass (such as black) is to be used both in the foreground and background, you can suggest depth by using a lighter value of glass, like dark gray, in the background or distant areas. This technique will also avoid making these dark areas in the back appear as holes in your picture.

Color tricks like these can be very effective. With a little know-how you can create an illusion of a door or hole that one could walk through.

Warm colors (reds, yellows, whites, oranges, golds) tend to come forward, while cool colors (blues, greens, violets, grays, silvers) recede. Psychologically, a room that is painted blue will feel cooler than one that is painted bright yellow. Cool colors suggest shadows; they seem transparent. Cool blues and greens are used to pull the viewer into the panel to create a place of refuge. Warm colors suggest light and seem more opaque. Hot reds and yellows stimulate the senses and demand attention. Sometimes the tension of mixing hot and cool colors gives just the right visual effect.

Distant parts of scenery, such as mountains, look bluish. Further back they appear grayish or violet; they also become smaller and hazy. Fresh snow in the foreground has a yellowish tint, bringing it closer to the viewer. It becomes grayer further away.

Sky near the horizon is a lighter blue than the deeper blue higher in the sky. The same is true of the ocean. Since the ocean reflects the sky, it is nearly the same color but varies in tone. The shore line appears a lighter blue than the darker water in the distance.

Luminosity

Color intensity (luminosity) is altered according to the color of the background. On a white background, light colors decrease in intensity. On a black background, light colors appear even lighter and more brilliant while dark ones diminish in intensity. Grays of the same value appear darker against a white background, and

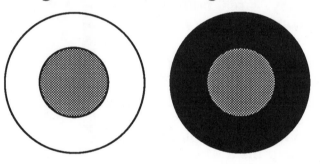

lighter against a black background. In the illustration, note that even though they appear different, the two grays are the same.

In the color chart, the series of orange triangles are graduated in size and placed on a background of blue (the complement of orange). You can see how luminosity increases in relation to size. In the first panel, where the triangle and background are equal in area, the orange and blue are equal in luminosity. In the last panel with the smallest triangle, the orange appears the most luminous of all.

Color perspective

There are two kinds of perspective, linear and color. Color perspective re-

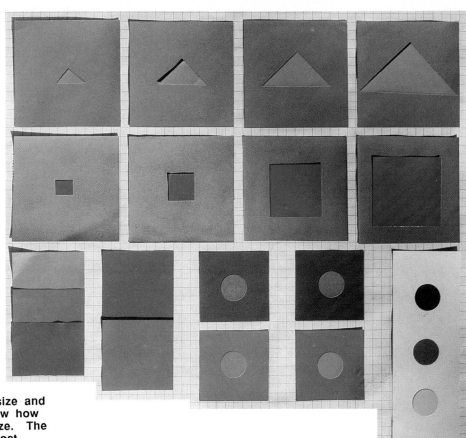

In the first two lines:

The orange triangles, graduated in size and placed on equal blue surfaces, show how luminosity increases in relation to size. The smallest triangle appears the most luminous. In the square with the largest triangle (equal in area) both the blue and the orange are equal in luminosity.

Non-complementary color schemes relate to one another differently. The large magenta square on the yellow background looks more purple than the smallest square, which seems more red-brown.

In the bottom line:

Two adjacent colors appear more alike if the transition from one to the other is gradual (first figure). The difference is accentuated by the use of a black dividing line. In stained glass, think of the black line as the seam line that heightens the contrast of two close shades of a color.

The disks appear different because of the contrast of the background. The disks on the darker background come forward while the disks on the lighter background recede.

Yellow (warm color) comes forward and appears larger. Blue (cool color) recedes and looks smaller. Light colors on a light background (yellow on white) become more brilliant, while dark colors on a light background diminish in intensity.

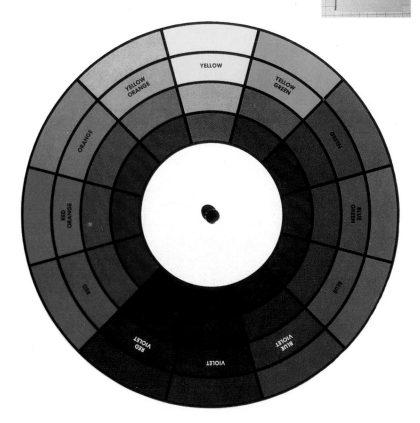

Color Wheel by permission of M. Grumbacher, Inc.

Upper left corner:

In the Chagall stained glass window, the focal point is in the upper right hand corner. The artist used cool shades of blue with the warm complements of red and orange to create depth. This window contains all the elements of good composition: repetition, variety, center of interest, unity, and balance.

Upper right corner:

Your personality should be evident in the style that you develop. This stained glass and metal panel and the remaining works on this page are by the author.

Lower left corner:

These stained glass bathroom shutter windows were planned to allow the design to flow from one to the other even though there is framing between.

Lower right corner:

Fused and stained glass panel illustrates linear perspective since the figures and umbrellas become smaller as they move closer to the horizon line.

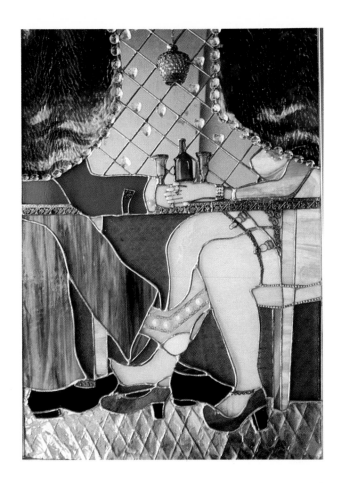

Line and Color Magic for Glass Design

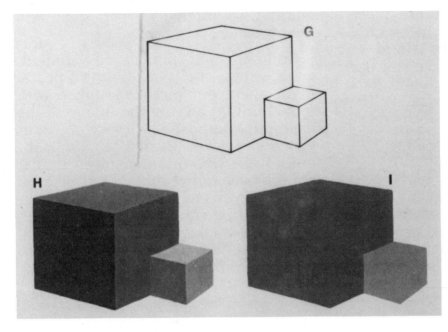

nations are disturbing and should be avoided. While harmony can be achieved by using analogous and complementary color schemes, value and intensity should be regulated through the size and position of the areas of color in the panel. Experimenting with the size and position of the dominant and subordinate colors with paper and markers will help you keep projects balanced.

fers to the optical, visual appearance of whatever the artist is trying to depict. Colors change as much as lines and shapes do, according to distance and form. In reality, everything is three-dimensional, and the artist must translate it to a two-dimensional plane. A figure, face or vase – every object has dimensional form that can be shaped through color shading. The roundness of an object is defined by the use of a darker value on its edges. For example, a round vase would be the brightest where it appears to be the closest. The sides would recede because they are shaded or darker, thus giving form to the vase.

Color balance and harmony

A harmonious color scheme is one in which hue, value, and intensity are pleasantly balanced. Extreme combi-

Phenomena

The eye detects the color of blue or yellow objects at a wider angle than the color of red or green objects. Because the edges of the retina do not register green and red effectively, these two colors should not be placed on the periphery of your panel. The viewer's eye should stay in the main framework of the picture.

Two adjacent colors appear more alike if the transition from one to the other is gradual. The difference is accentuated when the transition is sudden, as illustrated in the color plate in this chapter. The use of a black dividing line heightens the contrast of the two colors even if they are not that different. Similarly, black lines separating primary colors will cause a greater contrast between the colors.

If light colored objects are placed on a dark background, they seem to expand. They stand out and come forward. Conversely, if dark objects are placed on a light background, they seem to contract. They do not project forward, but recede and appear as holes in the background. See the color chart for examples.

Color value greatly affects the size and form of objects or areas depicted in a panel. A black circle on a dark gray background will appear larger than a black circle on a light gray background.

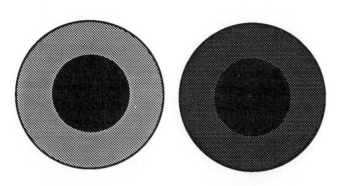

Colors which contrast too strongly, such as blue/red, blue/yellow , and red/green, can create illusions of shadows, vibrations, and after-images. Sometimes the results can be successful for special effects.

After-images

An after-image is the psychological, visual impression that takes place after the eye has been fixed on a color. It is the consequence of eye fatigue. If you gaze at a color for 20 or 30 seconds, and then look at a white background, you will see its complementary color (its exact opposite on the color wheel) within three to four sec-

onds at full intensity. The image will then fade.

Brilliant light persists as images, even when the source disappears. Right after your picture is taken with a flashbulb, you see the image of the flash superimposed on every object at which you gaze. Even after the flash-bulb circle has diminished so that it is no longer noticeable, it can be seen again if you look at a light background. If at that time you stare at a very dark background, the circle will appear in colors complementary to those seen on the white background.

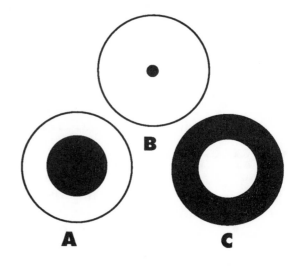

If you stare at Figure A for half a minute, then transfer your gaze to Figure B, a very white circle, whiter than background, will appear around the small dot in the center. Gazing at Figure C will cause an extremely dark circle to appear around the small dot in Figure B.

Hues of black and white also cause eye fatigue. As a result, after-images are produced.

It is important to realize that after-images affect color choices. Even if the colors are not unduly intense, after-images appear in the finished work. As the viewer gazes at the colors in the panel, the complementary colors are perceived. After-images help the viewer relate to the color scheme because they promote a complementary relationship. When one hue in a combination is stronger than any of the others, its after-image tends to give to the whole area a tone slightly complementary to the dominant hue.

Experiment III:

Place a small green circle on a white or light gray piece of paper. If you focus your eyes on it for 20 or 30 seconds, you will find that a reddish color appears to surround the edges of the green circle. If you focus your eyes a little to one side of the circle, you will see a faint image of the circle in red–the complement of green. You can try this experiment with other colors.

"As in all fields, perceiving color is probably a combination of natural talent, observing ability and, with the greatest artists, intuition."

Ralph Fabri

If you look out of the corner of your eye, you should see gray dots at the corners of the boxes.

OPTICAL ILLUSIONS

The two squares are the same size although the one that is pointing up and down appears larger.

The vertical line always appears longer than the horizontal.

The two horizontal lines are the same length, even though the line enclosed in the inverted brackets appears shorter.

The two horizontal lines appear to expand in the middle even though they are perfectly straight.

At a quick glance, the circle closer to the angle appears larger.

The lines are not slanted.

Chapter Six
BALANCING THE COMPOSITION

"(Composition is) the art of arranging, in a decorative manner, the various elements at the artist's disposal."

Henri Matisse

The artist uses the language of line symbols to communicate a desired image, a visual tool that conveys an idea. Design is the arrangement of objects or ideas in a pattern to produce an emotional effect. Each person interprets design differently. A unity of the design occurs when all of the following elements, as well as color and value, are integrated to form a visual, whole composition.

Essential elements create a unified composition

• **Line** - can suggest mass, mood, and energy. For instance, a curved line is considered soft or gentle. Oblique lines are dramatic. Scribbled or wavy lines suggest motion.

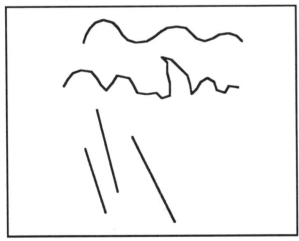

• **Size, Shape, or Form** - everything has a shape, obvious or subtle: geometric, circular, or irregular. Shapes should vary in size. The positioning and balance of these shapes is an important element.

• **Center of Interest** - object or shape that is more dominant than any other. Emphasizing a dominant area is discussed later in this chapter.

• **Texture** - can create space and interest. In glass, there are unlimited textures, both on the surface and within the glass, to weave through a composition.

• **Suggestive Space** - through color and line, creates depth by overlapping, relative size, and perspective.

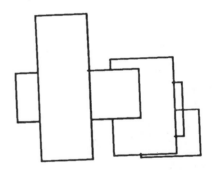

Each of the above elements should possess the following:

rhythm
repetition
variety
unity
balance

• **Rhythm** - Rhythmic recurrences in a composition hold the viewer's attention while the eye moves to connect the images. Rhythm occurs when similar elements are repeated at regular and recognizable intervals in alternating or sequenced patterns.

This composition illustrates rhythm and repetition with similar elements, shape and position.

• **Variety** - Interest can be aroused by varying sizes, shapes, colors, and contrasts. Different size lead or copper foil seams, as well as glass shapes, can create variety.

• **Repetition** - Shape, position, density, color, or texture can be repeated and will provide a feeling of security and order because of their inherent logic.

• **Unity** - Line, color, shape, size, and position should relate to one another in an orderly fashion. All the elements should look as if they belong in the same panel. Masses should be connected by common shapes or color.

• **Balance** - A work of art can either be symmetrical (same on both sides) or asymmetrical (out of balance). Balance can encompass texture, color, and pattern as well as line.

Balancing act

Balance is maintained visually through symmetrical, asymmetrical, or radial equilibrium.

• **Symmetry** creates a mirror effect. It occurs when every mass on one side of the center of a work is duplicated exactly on the other side of a central axis, horizontally and/or vertically. A symmetrical work is formal, stable, and passive. Al-

This wall panel illustrates variety: size of glass and lead lines, shapes, color and contrast; yet all elements relate to one another.

Line and Color Magic for Glass Design

though a symmetrical panel is easier to plan and has an inherent logic, the finished work can be dull and uninteresting.

When the design and details are exactly the same on both sides, the composition is symmetrical.

• **Asymmetrical** balance occurs when masses are not identical, but counterbalanced and pleasing to the eye because of the feel of the combined weight distribution. Asymmetrical compositions are energetic and informal. Asymmetrical balance can be achieved by varying the elements (size, shape, form, texture, etc.) and placement.

• **Radial** equilibrium is usually thought of as a circular balance, emanating from a central point instead of a cen-

tral line. Visual components lead from the point; a wheel with spokes is a good example.

Balance can be understood if you think of balancing objects on an ordinary weighing scale. If they weigh the same amount, objects on either side of the scale will cause the scale to balance. If the objects are unequal in weight, the scale can also be made to balance; the lighter weight must be moved farther from the center of the scale than the heavier weight. Please refer to photo D.

When designing a panel, however, you are working with lines and colors, not weights. Lines define objects in a composition, and values and colors give weight to the objects. In the illustration in photo A, see how the landscape is unbalanced due to the clump

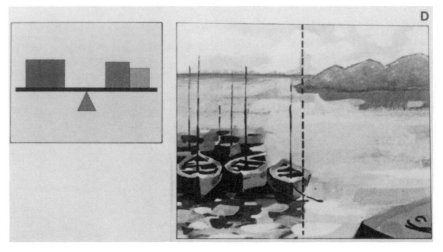

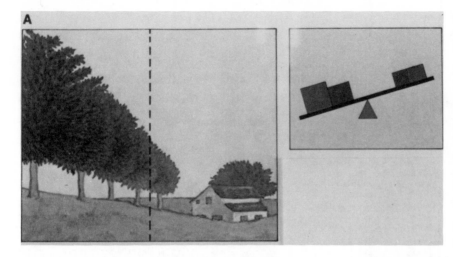

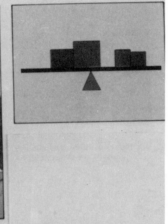

ues appear heavier than lighter values. These must be balanced as well. In Van Gogh's *Starry Night* shown below, you can see how balance is achieved through light and dark values. The eye is drawn through the painting because these values suggest movement. This painting is also a good example of a successful entrance and exit.

Enter stage left

Since reading is done from left to right, lines from the left draw the eye into a composition. Lines sloping down on the right tend to lead the eye out. The left is stronger than the right; it

of trees on the left. In photo B, shifting the large mass of trees toward the center gives a better balance between one side and the other. It might be helpful to take an imaginary line vertically through the center of your design to evaluate if the masses seem balanced on both sides. An imaginary horizontal line through the center will determine if the design has four-sided symmetry.

As illustrated in the "Color Power" chapter, darker val-

seems able to carry more weight. The viewer tends to look at the left side of a plane first, assuming that it has greater importance.

In a composition, there should be one area that immediately attracts the eye. This is the starting point for the viewer and should lead the eye to further exploration. If the picture has deep perspective, the best entry is through a series of curves or zigzags, since it is easy for the eye to follow a line, especially a long receding one

that draws the viewer into the picture. This technique is used often in landscape subjects where the focal point is often in the central distance.

This concept also applies to a figure or portrait. A left profile seems to be looking toward the viewer. A right profile seems to be looking away from the viewer. A running figure facing left and positioned close to the left side of the panel seems to run into the edge. A running figure headed left and positioned at the right edge of the panel appears to back out of the picture. See below.

This composition appears to have great depth. The viewer's eye follows the zigzag steps to a central focal point.

Exit stage right

How the eye exits a picture is just as important as how the eye enters it. If the viewer enters the picture by means of curves or zigzags, the eye should be drawn out of the picture by the same kind of line. The sketch shown here is a good example of how the eye flows in and out of a composition. The overlapping clouds which start on the left hand side gently slope to the right hand side. The angle of the rolling waves leads the eye to travel into the picture and out on the right where the sky and waves are close together.

The eye enters from the lower left of a panel and exits out through the right side.

You may have to experiment with lines to see what object or accent in your panel would lead the eye away from the focal point and out of the composition.

Directions in compositions

Just as line can suggest mood, the direction of a composition can imply movement or energy flow. Directional movements can be horizontal, vertical, triangular, diagonal, curved, circular, or combinations.

A horizontal composition gives a sense of flat space and depth.Although it is considered more static and restful, it can be used for striking effects. Sub-

jects that lend themselves to this type of arrangement are still life, land or sea scapes.

A vertical composition gives a sense of up and down movement. It is very forceful and must be offset with other elements. For example, a forest landscape with vertical trees might need some large branches flowing horizontally.

The diagonal movement is a powerful direction and will pull the viewer's attention up and down and across the composition. This type of composition can be dramatic even though the lines may be subtle.

There is less feeling of depth in a horizontal composition.

Line and Color Magic for Glass Design

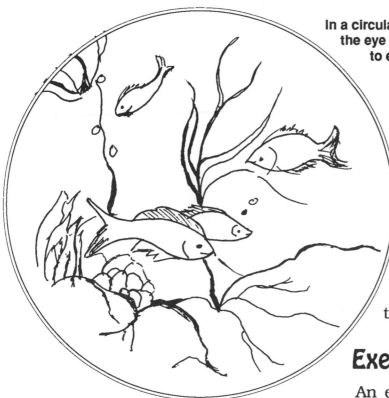

surrounding the positive shapes are the negative spaces. The positive space is one which is usually centrally located and stands out in the composition.

The negative space should be interestingly broken up into smaller areas. Negative space in glass art can act as important rest areas for the eye. These spaces can be broken up with glass cut lines or enhanced by using varied textures of glass.

The circular composition is unbroken and has a continuous flow that symbolizes completeness. Glass panels constructed as circles and ovals are successful because they are complete shapes with no beginning or end.

A triangular composition, which can be off-center or centered, suggests a stable movement. When each side of the triangle is balanced, it creates a feeling of solidity.

Positive & negative space

The positive space in a composition is the main subject matter. This might consist of shapes of the objects or persons, trees, flowers. The areas

Exercise:

An exercise that will enable you to become more aware of negative space is to draw five or more similar shapes on a piece of paper. Place them in an eye-appealing arrangement. Draw the grouping so that the space surrounding is in proportion to the subject matter. Using carbon paper, duplicate your drawing. Cut the copy, separating the grouping from the background. Observe the remaining negative space. Does it make an in-

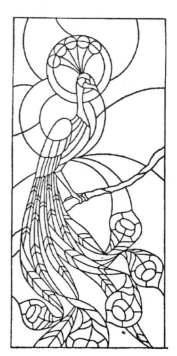

The peacock is positive space; surrounding is negative space interestingly broken up with complementary flowing cut lines. Design by Muriel Caffee.

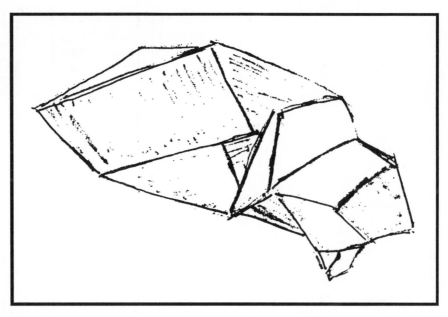

teresting design of its own? On the intact drawing, make pencil lines in the negative areas to designate as glass cut lines. These lines should flow with the design. Create patterns that encourage the viewer to use these cut lines to guide the eye in and around the composition.

In complicated compositions, such as a landscape, it might be more difficult to distinguish the positive and negative spaces. The positive areas contain the more important elements that draw the eye, whereas the lesser (without detail) spaces are the negative or eye rest areas.

"...All composition is order of one kind or another."

John Canaday

This is a sketch by a student in the author's design workshop.

Chapter Seven
POINT OF VIEW

When drawing or designing, you create a separate reality with graphic representations of line and color. By understanding the scientific theory of how the eye and mind translate these images, you become better equipped to express yourself artistically. What you see is not always what actually exists. Lines and colors can affect one another and create ambiguous messages. Lines can easily fool the mind into misinterpretations of size, length, and spatial relationships. It is important to know about perspective, line, illusion, and focal point to enable you to send your message while creating dynamic art.

Draw the line

"Line may be used for its own sake, or as the defining edge of a shape, or as a structural or expressive device."
John Canaday

Crooked, jagged lines suggest stress.

A line is expressive. It sets a mood, conveys energy, and delivers a message. A straight line suggests tranquility or rigidity, while a crooked, jagged line suggests stress. A curved line represents movement or fluidity.

The vertical line is stronger than the horizontal, and it usually appears longer than it really is. The vertical line is more important than any other because it is the first seen by the eye. The horizontal line denotes

The eye can be fooled by optical illusions. Top left–The dots and circles express motion. Top right–Which do you see first–the circle or the diamond? Bottom–The vertical lines are straight even though they appear crooked.

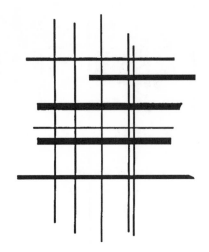

Vertical lines are stronger than horizontal. Straight lines suggest repose.

An illusion of movement is created: repetition of rotating circles, overlapping forms, balancing warm & cool colors. The eye follows a rhythmic path through the composition.

stillnness and suggests repose. A longer, thicker line becomes more dominant that a shorter, thinner line.

A slanted or oblique line suggests movement more than a vertical or horizontal line. Zigzags, straight intersecting lines, and rotating circles also suggest motion. Movement can also be implied by repetition of shape, overlapping forms, linear perspective, or balancing warm and cool colors.

Creating an illusion of movement helps the viewer connect the shapes while moving the eye through a rhythmic path. These inferred spatial techniques will be more powerful if designed with the elements described in the previous chapter: variety, rhythm, texture, balancing non-complementary and complementary colors, etc. These techniques are used by artists to command attention, compelling the observer to linger and examine the creation.

Perspective

A realistic composition must represent a third dimension: depth. In order to create the illusion of depth, an artist uses perspective. The effect of distance is created by gradually changing the tones of color and the strength of the line. The object nearest to the observer is drawn in sharp, heavy lines and dark color. Faint lines and light colors seem to make objects fade into the distance. This concept is called aerial perspective.

Linear perspective is based on the idea that an item will appear smaller in size as the distance between it and the observer grows greater. A ship seems to grow smaller as it sails

Line and Color Magic for Glass Design

Distance is created when strength of colors and lines diminish in the distance.

picture plane. When objects are positioned at the viewer's eye level, neither the tops nor the bottoms of planes are seen. If the eye level changes, the horizon line is altered. As a standing observer is seated, the horizon line moves up; if the observer stands, the line moves down. The observer will see the bottom of objects when he or she is positioned below the horizon line; when positioned above the horizon line, the observer will see the top of objects. Lines above the horizon appear to slope down toward it, while lines below the horizon appear to lead up toward it.

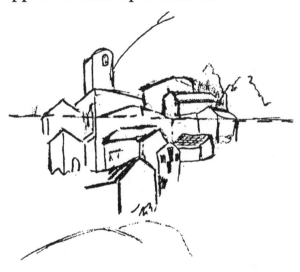

away. In the fused and stained glass panel pictured in the color section, the figures and umbrellas become smaller as they move closer to the horizon line. Please refer to the color section for this photograph. If several objects of the same size stand at different distances from the observer, they will appear to be different sizes. A good example is a line of telephone poles. Linear perspective also includes the principle that parallel lines recede as they seem to converge at one point. In a view of a long straight highway, the sides of the road appear to meet at a point on the horizon. Note: vertical lines remain vertical.

The eye level of the observer determines the location of the horizon line, which runs horizontally across the

You can create depth by overlapping, a powerful spatial technique. Overlapping occurs when one form appears to be in front or overlaying another, partially hiding it, such as clouds or trees which vary in size and shape.

Focal point

Most paintings or panels should have a center of interest. Every item in a picture has some degree of at-

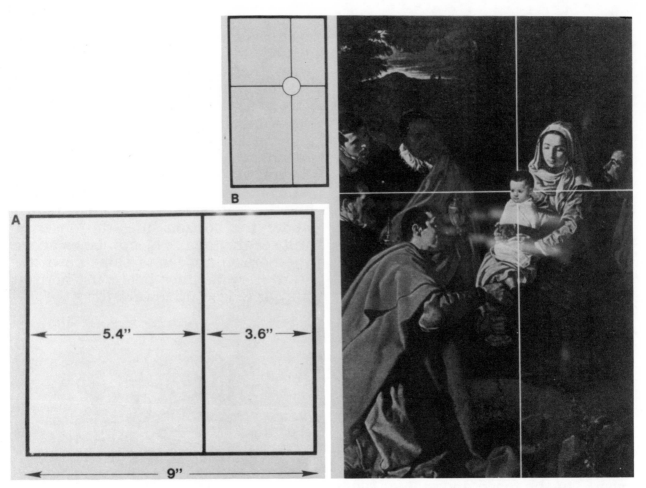

Some artists use the "Golden Section Principle" to determine where to place the focal point.

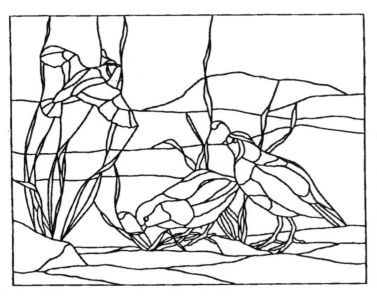

Avoid placing the focal point in the center of a panel. Pattern by Muriel Caffee.

traction; however, one feature should dominate to become the center of interest. In every composition the eye should cross the focal point at least once. Because the center is uninteresting, a focal point should never be placed there unless it is a symmetrical design. In the Chagall glass painting pictured in the color section, the focal point is placed in the upper right hand section.

To determine where to place a center of interest, many artists use a theory of art from ancient Greece called the

"Golden Section Principle." By multiplying the height and width of your panel by 0.6, you can section off your design at a ratio of three to five.

For example, the figure shown here is a 9" wide rectangle. Because 9" multiplied by 0.6 equals 5.4", one section will equal 5.4". Subtract 5.4" from the original 9" to find the second section: 3.6". Multiplying both the width and the height by 0.6 will help you find an effective place for a focal point.

Proportion may be determined intuitively or by means of mathematical ratio or progression. Although mathematics and nature hold infinite possibilities, the artist must depend on intuitive sense or a feeling for the rightness of the relationship. By testing, observing, and comparing, you can sharpen your feeling for proportion.

What you get is not what you see

• A unit or object in the foreground has less weight than an identical unit in the background.

• A larger form is stronger and will attract the eye quicker than a smaller form.

• Regular and closed forms are more dominant than irregular and open ones.

• A solid form is stronger than one which is diffused.

• A group of attached shapes is not as powerful as an isolated shape.

• A form which is centered is not as powerful as a form which is off-center, particularly one located in the upper part of a composition, the right side, or at a distance in space.

• Forms or shapes of unusual intricacy and unique relationships are strong.

• Objects that are positioned lower in a picture appear closer and darker.

Experiment

Take two pieces of white paper; cut one in half. Draw a small box of the same size on both pieces. Look at the box on the larger sheet of paper. It will seem smaller than the box on the half page.

The organizing mind

The mind tends to organize what the eye sees. Some of the visual clues that influence these organizational tendencies should be mentioned.

• The closer that visual elements are to each other, the more they are grouped together perceptually.

• The more clearly the forms follow a regular and predictable pattern, the more they are perceived as single, unified groups.

• The more the forms indicate enclosed spaces, the more they are perceived as complete forms.

• The more the forms correspond to

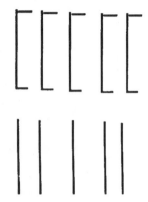

one another in shape, size, direction, color, or other characteristics, the more they are linked together perceptually.

Forms in this panel relate to one another in shape, size, direction and color.

With the medium of glass, another design factor should be considered. Due to the refraction of light changing during the day, the dominant form or color can shift. The relationship between transparent and opalescent glass will also affect the impact of your finished panel.

The size of an object or form is relative to that which it is being compared. Images or elements of similar size tend to compete for attention. One of the forms should be emphasized through texture, shape, size, or color so that the eye will choose a dominant object.

• One lone line or object will be more dominant than a group of lines or objects.

• An object centrally located will attract more attention than one that is

Stare at the center of this drawing, as the lines seem to be swirling into the center hole. Lines can express movement.

closer to the edges of a panel.

• Less important figures should be placed near the edge of the panel.

• Borders can help contain a subject. A glass panel or picture that incorporates a border encloses the subject, ensuring the attention of the viewer within the framework.

"Line is one of the fundamental tools in art. Line can suggest mass, texture, light and shadow. It can have its own character, from an irregular scribble to a smooth curve."

J. M. Parramon

Perspective in review

Borders help contain a subject as illustrated in this fused glass panel.

A simple method of learning how to draw things in perspective is to draw the horizon line (your eye level) first. Lines meet the vanishing point on the horizon line. All vertical lines remain vertical.

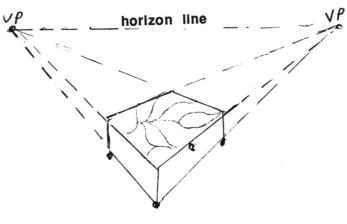

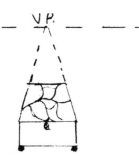

Above - One point perspective: you see only the top and front of the box. Lines meet at one point on the horizon line.

Top Right - Two point perspective: you see the side, front, and top of the box. Lines go out to meet the vanishing points on the outer edges of the horizon line.

Bottom Right - Three point perspective: Looking down on a skyscraper, you see the top and sides of the building. Horizontal lines go out to meet the vanishing points. Notice that window and door lines go the same way.

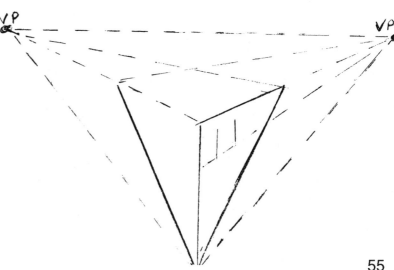

55

VISUAL MAGIC SUMMARY

	Strong	Weak
Contrast	high contrasts	low contrasts
Shape	closed shapes regular shapes	open shapes irregular shapes
Size	larger shapes	smaller shapes
Density	solid shapes	unfilled shapes
Position	off-center shapes	centered shapes
Environment	isolated shapes	grouped shapes
Form	intricate shapes unique shapes	simple shapes common shapes
Lines	vertical lines oblique lines	horizontal lines

	Recede from the Viewer	Approach the Viewer
Colors	dark values cool colors	light values warm colors
Lines	thin lines	thick lines
Shapes	small shapes	large shapes
Sizes	small sizes	large sizes
Textures	smooth textures	rough textures

Chapter Eight
DRAW OUT YOUR CREATIVITY

"No great artist ever sees things as they really are. If he did he would cease to be an artist."

Oscar Wilde

Some craftspersons do not need a pattern to accomplish a project. Some measure off glass to suit their needs or assemble glass like a collage. Others purchase commercial patterns or trace from a pattern book. However, for those who would like to design patterns but do not have the confidence to draw, this chapter will present exercises often used to teach drawing skills.

Each person conceives and expresses a different viewpoint.

Mountain scenes can appear dramatically different.

Kick-start your designing ability

Sketching can be fun if you do it for yourself; don't worry about what other people think of your work. Loosen up. Use any kind of white paper and soft pencil or charcoal with free, light movements of the hand and arm. The following sketching exercise will help extract imaginative designs, stimulate your creativity, and get you out of your mind-set.

Sketch three different versions of one of the symbols listed below. Do not sketch in your learned, accepted, traditional method, but attempt to use alternate or out-of-the-ordinary depictions and arrangements. Do not be concerned with details and color. Keep in mind that there is no right or wrong way to draw something. It can be your own interpretation. For instance, the hats could be bizarre expressions with wild feathers and fairy tale flowers. You could draw one or several, parts or in total, abstractly or realistically. Draw the objects from a unique viewpoint, for example, from the back or inside. Try to make each of the three sketches totally different, thus stretching your capacity to express ideas uniquely. It is important to relinquish preconceived ideas and see things with renewed vision.

The following list is suggested subject matter:

hats	the sun
windows	leaves
sacks and bags	houses

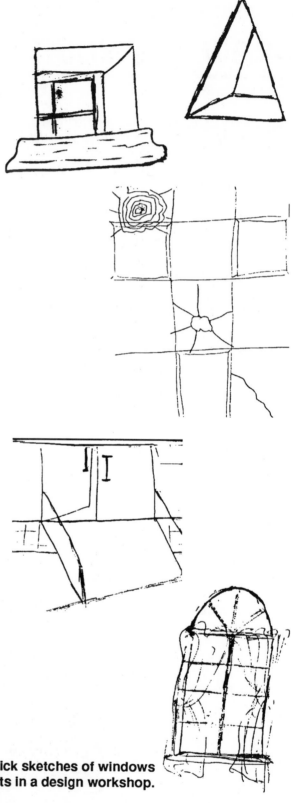

The illustrations shown are examples of quick sketches of windows drawn by the author's students in a design workshop.

Graph paper and rulers

Another kick-start method that works well for some is to begin with a ruler and 8 1/2" x 11" quarter-inch graph paper. The visual lines serve as a guide, especially for geometric shapes. If you are inexperienced with drafting designs, begin by drawing several small-scaled rectangular designs, moving the ruler from point to point. Line off interesting geometric patterns, such as diamond shapes, rectangles, squares, triangles, etc. Using graph paper helps you think in terms of good, logical, proportional design.

Drafting and art stores carry interesting rulers that can help you design curves. Flex-curves and french rulers can even suggest linear designs. French rulers come in a set of three and have all kinds of intricate curves. The lamp and cabinet doors pictured here were designed with french rulers.

Abstract designing exercise

The Rorschach test is a method used by some artists to design abstract compositions. Many people have difficulty drawing an abstract pattern.

On 8 1/2" X 11" paper, drop small quantities of colored ink or water colors in the center of the page. Fold the paper in half. Open the paper and study the design. Turn it around and see if you find a pattern that would make an interesting abstract. It might encompass the entire painting or only a portion of it.

Where to draw the line

To practice drawing, use pencil, pen, ink, marker, charcoal, or even crayon. Get the feel of the one most comfortable for you. Sketch quickly with large sweeps of your entire arm and eliminate insignificant details.

To draw an object, person, or scene, you must be very familiar with it. Most artists are unable to draw an item without studying it. If someone asked you to sketch a dog from memory, the chances are that you could not do it unless you had practiced or had drawn one before.

When you draw from real life, use simple shapes such as circles, cones, squares, or triangles to represent forms. Translating images into these basic shapes makes the drawing task easier, as shown below.

As you sketch, be aware of the negative space or rest areas you are creating. Positive and negative space was discussed in Chapter Six.

Continuous line exercise

To encourage your subconscious mind to take over while sketching, try this continuous line exercise. Tape down a piece of paper to your work surface. Place an object, such as a telephone, next to you. While studying the object, draw it with one continuous line without lifting your pencil from the paper. Do not look at the paper, but let your hand receive the message from your brain. Don't be concerned if your drawing is not a reasonable facsimile. Your drawings will improve as you practice this exercise, and it will also strengthen your ability to observe details.

Keep it in perspective

The theory of perspective was discussed in detail in the previous chapter. Now it's time to learn how!

Everything has dimension. When drawing, you translate three-dimensional objects and images into two dimensions. You can give the illusion of depth by drawing horizontal lines at angles. What you see at eye level is the horizon line. Lines converge downward or upward on an angle to meet the eye level. Vertical lines always remain straight up and down at a 90 degree angle. It is only the horizontal lines or angled lines which change.

Foresight is better than hindsight

Sighting is a method to help you visually judge size and perspective and draw by eye. Find an object to draw, such as a table or dresser. Extending your arm forward, hold a pencil horizontally at exact eye level. Close one eye to estimate angles and line direction, Compare the horizon-

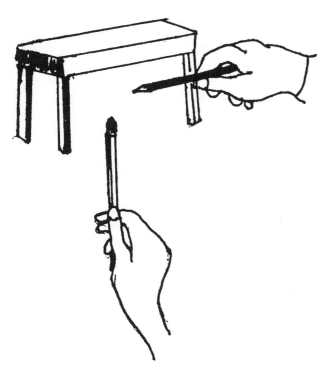

tal angles to the horizontal line of your pencil. Now draw the same angle in relation to the top or bottom of your paper. For the vertical angles, hold your pencil once again at eye level, one eye closed. Compare the vertical angle to the line of the pencil. Now draw the same angle in relation to the sides of your paper.

Sighting can be used to determine length and width. Holding your pencil in the same manner, align one end of the pencil to the edge of the line you want to measure. Use your thumb on the pencil to indicate the length of the line. Move the pencil to other lines, comparing one line size to the other. See illustration.

To get a feeling for drawing perspective, practice sketching boxes at different eye levels both above and below the horizon line. Place the box on the floor or on a table, then place it on a high shelf. After you feel confident drawing an opaque box, a clear plastic cube can be used to give you the opportunity to see through to the lines on the other side.

Sketching a landscape or seascape

If you are drawing a landscape, eliminate not only detail but also some of the view to simplify it. To reduce visual perception, some artists squint or look through a viewfinder. This is an aid to help define your composition. A viewfinder can easily be made by cutting a square hole in the middle of a piece of square cardboard. Your drawing can be representational (close to reality), or stylized (exaggerated lines). Draw only what is essential to express your vision.

• Define the limits of your view.

• Establish your horizon line, which is your eye level.

• Draw the horizon line lightly across the drawing as a reference point. A landscape horizon line should be low, to allow space to create depth.

Cut lines in a glass panel should follow the flow of the design. Note: idea originated from a postcard.

Tricks and tools

A reducing glass, available from art stores, helps you look at your drawing as a whole to see if your composition is balanced and in perspective. It does the opposite of a magnifying glass since it reduces your design, giving you a total view. It can be helpful for designing any subject matter where you need to focus in on the whole picture.

When your drawing is finished, turn it upside down and to its side. The composition and positive/negative space should be as interesting from any view.

Designing a pattern for stained glass

An important consideration when drawing a pattern for stained glass is the cutting factor and reinforcing. You must think of the cut lines or reinforcing as part of the total design concept. The seam lines should repeat the same type of lines, such as curves, zigzags, or geometrics. Seams should not be obtrusive but be continuous lines flowing from objects such as buildings, flowers, or tree branches. These could extend to the end of a panel.

Reinforcement of a large panel is important, especially if there are large glass pieces that do not intersect. A panel with smaller pieces of glass will have more seam joints and is stronger than a panel with large sections. Long rectangular pieces of glass in a panel have a tendency to break if not handled properly.

Reinforcing wire is available to solder in the seams of panels which need to take abuse because they will be taken to galleries or shows. Framing helps to strengthen panels that are under four to six square feet.

However, anything larger than this should have some type of reinforcement within the design pieces.

Smaller pieces are reinforced by intersecting soldered joints and reinforcing rods.

The design of two or three panels positioned next to each other (windows, cabinets, or shutter doors) can be identical or they can be planned so that the design appears as one scene. Even though there is framing between the panels, the eye will see it as one composition. See the two concepts pictured on the next page.

When designing your glass art, allow your individuality to be evident. Let your personality come through and dominate the theme. Develop a style that is uniquely yours. If your work is for sale, create a series of work in either the same color scheme, mode, or theme.

Not a 9-to-5 job

Some people create projects for a definite purpose. Motivation speeds up the creative process. Sometimes the strongest impetus is the pressure of a time deadline. People who react to this form of motivation usually subconsciously "arrange" such a situation for themselves. These people will procrastinate, knowing that they work better under pressure. If motivation is your problem, erase your negative attitude by visualizing your completed project and the joy that the creative process brings.

Your excitement can be easily diminished by the distraction of clutter. Following each work day, clean your studio so that your working space is organized. This way you will have a fresh start and feel eager to begin, an important step if one is to retain enthusiasm.

Take frequent work breaks. Stretching and walking exercises change the body's chemistry. Exercise refreshes the mind, allowing you to renew your creative energy.

Techniques can be learned, but it is only with much practice that drawing skills can improve. So be confident and try to sketch frequently.

"Ideas are the roots of creation."
Ernest Dimnet

When designing two or three panels next to one another, allow the design to flow through even though there might be framing between them.

Chapter nine

ALTERING THE SIZE OF YOUR DESIGN

"Always design a thing by considering it in its next larger context."

E. Saarinen

Often you will find an appealing design or interesting pattern from an unrelated source. The design would translate beautifully to a glass project, but it is not the right size. This chapter will show you how to change dimensions to fill a particular need or to suit your aesthetic sense.

In selecting your design, be aware that its impact may be altered dramatically by enlargement. Conversely, its impact may be diminished by a change in scale. You may want to use only a portion of a design.

Make three or four photocopies of your original small design to be used as color renderings. These will be most helpful in selecting colors and textures of glass. Color these designs with markers or crayons to use for comparison purposes. Color selection will be discussed in depth in a later chapter.

The preceding chapter on creativity discussed the fact that you need not be an artist to conceive a design for a glass project. There are relatively few people with the ability to draw a design freehand to scale. Most do well to sketch a small pattern that can be enlarged by mechanical means such as a pantograph, opaque projector, or slide projector. Another method of enlarging a design is to scale it by using various sizes of graph paper.

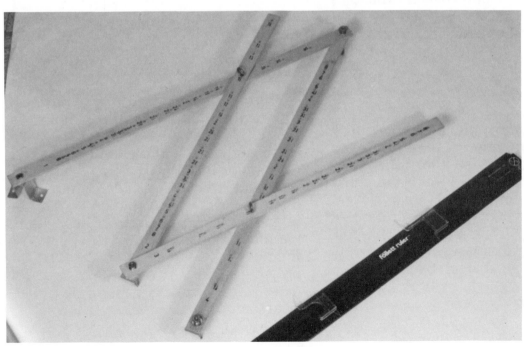

A
Follett
Ruler
and a
Pantograph

A small drawing can be enlarged by various methods including the use of a pantograph, opaque projector, computer, or slide projector.

These methods will serve you well in enlarging a small design culled from another source, such as a book, advertisement, or greeting card.

Pantograph

The pantograph, available from most art supply stores, is an inexpensive and easy-to-use tool for scaling drawings. It is a set of intersecting rulers, one end fitted with a lead point and the other with a scribe used to trace the original pattern. The pantograph is adjustable and can be used to enlarge or decrease the size of a design.

Opaque projector

The opaque projector is a more sophisticated and accurate enlarging method than the pantograph. The original drawing is placed on a "stage" under the lamp of the projector. The enlarged image is projected onto pattern paper fastened to a wall. Tracing of the enlarged pattern is now a simple matter of drawing in the portion of the design you wish to utilize. Opaque projectors are available in various price ranges from glass supply houses or art shops.

Proportion wheel

The proportion wheel, available from art craft or graphics sources, calculates the dimensions to scale up or scale down a pattern. The proportion wheel consists of two imprinted (ruled) discs of different sizes, fixed to rotate upon each other. The smaller disc indicates the size of the original. Move the smaller disc on the top to line up with the size (number) of the desired dimension on the lower, larger disc. When the two sizes are aligned you will be able to read the proportion of increase or decrease as

An Opaque Projector and a Slide Projector

Slide projector

The slide projector is another way to enlarge patterns, and many people already own a 35 mm. slide projector. Take a photo of your small freehand sketch using slide film and have it made into a transparency. Slides taken of scenery or events, such as a circus or boating race, can be projected on the drawing paper fastened to the wall.

In both of these methods, the size of your projected image is determined by the distance between the projector and the wall. Distortion of the image is also possible, if desired, by tilting the picture on the projector.

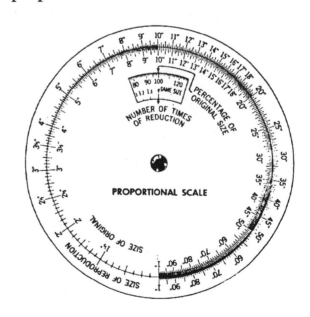

a percentage in a window on the smaller disc.

Once you know the percentage of your increase/decrease, it is much easier to choose the appropriate grid paper to chart out your design. If you use a copy shop to enlarge your design, you will be able to request the exact percent of the enlargement.

Graph paper

The square grid (graph paper) method is commonly used by craftspeople to enlarge or reduce. The design is first traced onto graph paper with small grids and then drawn, freehand, square by square, onto graph paper with larger grids. Each line that is drawn in the small square must be duplicated in the larger square. If you originally use 1/4 inch grid and transfer it to one-inch grid, your design will be enlarged by four.

Grid paper, available in many grid sizes (four to the inch, five to the inch, eight to the inch, etc.), can be purchased in a variety of sheet sizes. It is also available in rolls. Unprinted transparent paper can be used over acetate grids, enabling you to transfer your design to plain paper.

A light box or a glass–topped table with a light source beneath is helpful when tracing a design.

Plate divider paper

Plate divider paper is heavy bond with divisions for designing twelve-inch plate patterns. It can also aid in designing circular panels. This paper can be obtained at a ceramic, craft, or art supply store.

Transfer paper

Used like carbon paper, transfer paper is a one-step tracing method for transferring a design on glass. It comes in several

Graph Paper, Plate Divider, French Curves, Flex Ruler, and Compass are pictured.

colors, including graphite. It is excellent to use on mirror or dark colored glass. The lines disappear completely during glass firing. A sewing, ceramic, or craft supply store carries transfer paper.

Follett ruler

The Follett ruler is an accurate method of enlarging or reducing patterns without the use of graph paper. The ruler can also change the proportions of a design to fit any required space. Through the use of a sliding pointer, the device is used to mark off horizontal or vertical divisions within a pattern, forming a grid. An original design can be drafted easily after identifying the divisions upon which the design is based. There are two different rulers: one divides into halves, the other into thirds.

Computer

While the computer is the "design tool" of the future, it is now being used as a means to create, distort, enlarge, and reduce designs. Although you may not have access to a computer in your home studio, you should be aware of the advantages to be enjoyed by working with computer programs. Some software programs currently available are:

Adobe Illustrator	Colorix (VGA Paint)
CorelDraw	EGA Paint
MacDraw	Deluxe Paint II
Superpaint	Designer

A scanner picks up images from newspapers, photographs, etc. and produces them on the monitor screen. The images can be altered by using some of the enlargement, reduction, distortion, or reversal features of the particular software program. You can literally "play with" or recreate the image on the screen. It is often possible to come up with ideas and designs that are computer-generated.

There are photocopy, graphic, and printing establishments which can enlarge and duplicate your small drawing for a reasonable fee. It might be worth your time to investigate this possibility for very large pieces.

"A creative artist works on his next composition because he was not satisfied with his previous one."

Dmitri Shostakovich

**Drawing a small design on graph paper and enlarging
it by the methods described in this chapter
is easier than drawing a life-size design.**

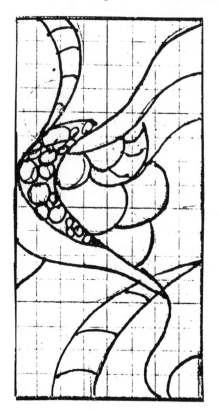

Line and Color Magic for Glass Design

Chapter Ten

GLASS: WHAT'S IN A NAME

"This is the garden: colors come and go."

e. e. cummings

Glass, an ancient, mysterious substance, presents an ever-changing spectrum of dancing color and reflection that uses light to perform its ballet. Styles, methods, and color preferences in stained glass art have changed from century to century. In the 15th Century, artisans used a formula for working out the proportions of their designs. The formula required the use of five pieces of white or clear glass, two pieces of blue, and one piece of red. Much of the glass of that time was painted.

Contemporary glass artisans are fortunate to have the availability of a wide selection of glass, modern equipment, and information about techniques. Crafters have an advantage in working with stained glass as an art medium because color and texture are its intrinsic characteristics.

Even if you are unfamiliar with many basic color fundamentals, you will find that most glass blends and coordinates well together. Take a tip from nature--even a lush garden blooming in a profusion of colors can present a harmonious, balanced composition. The wide range of unique textures, patterns, and exquisite glass colors radiate and refract light, making it an exciting medium to explore. The craft lends itself to numerous glass art techniques.

Stained Glass has become the modern term for the industry, the craft, and the art. It can also refer to any kind of object made by joining glass with metal strips. Stained glass itself is thought of as colored flat glass. There are two basic types of stained glass: machine-made glass in transparent and opal and the more costly hand-blown glass referred to as antique glass.

Sandblasting is carving, shading, or texturizing a glass surface. Sand or abrasive substance is blasted with high pressure air from special equipment. A design is created in clear, flashed, or mirror glass.

Fusing is melting layers of glass together by means of heat, usually a kiln. Fusible glass is manufactured by several companies for this purpose.

Just my type

Hand-blown glass, desirable because of its intense colors, has a faceted quality and is used by many professional studios. Its thickness and texture vary, and it comes in sheets smaller than machine-made glass. Hand-blown glass is very easy to cut.

Machine-made glass is more economical and readily available. It comes in a wide range of beautiful colors and textures. Reds and oranges are usually more expensive due to the addition of precious materials in the manufacturing process.

Textured glasses are manufactured through a double-roll forming process, producing a material smooth on one side and textured on the other. A number of different textured effects are available, but the most common are granite and hammered.

There are many other types of glass that can be used to create exciting art objects. Commercial and architectural glass of various types, such as frosted, ribbed, fluted, plate, embossed, and mirror, can be combined for exciting results.

Relatives in the art glass family

There is an infinite variety of glass from which the stained glass artist can choose:

• **Baroque Glass** - a swirling linear patterned glass available in several colors. It is attractive for traditional subjects.

• **Beveled Glass** - usually clear, has polished, cut, angled edges which produce light refracted through prisms. There are many shaped and patterned bevels. Beveled doors are very much in vogue today.

• **Cathedral Glass** - a single color, manufactured in sheets, smooth on both sides with no texture.

• **Catspaw Glass** - appears that a cat has walked across the surface and left its paw prints.

• **Crackle Glass** - small cracks appear to run through the glass, resembling alligator skin.

• **Drapery Glass** - heavily textured glass that resembles drapery. Great for special effects.

• **Flashed Glass** - antique glass that is clear or light-colored with a thin layer of color on one side. The thin colored layer can be sandblasted, revealing the base color or clear glass in a pattern.

• **Fracture-Streamers Glass** - colored threads of glass cascading over a clear, textured base sheet embedded

Fracture-Streamers Glass, Glue Chip Glass, and Catspaw Glass

with chips of soft pastel.

• **Glue-Chip Glass** - pattern resembles a fern, available in limited colors. Often used for background.

• **Iridescent Glass** - resembles an oily, metallic film of soft color on water producing a rainbow effect. Used sparingly, iridescent glass can elegantly enhance all types of projects.

• **Mirror** - effects change depending on daylight, night, and light source. Mirrors are available in various thicknesses and colors to use for sandblasting or stained glass art projects.

• **Opalescent Glass** - One, two, or three colors are combined with white during the manufacturing process to produce a swirled or streaked effect. Translucency varies depending on manufacture. This semi-transparent glass lends itself for lamp shades.

• **Reamy Glass** - wavy surface with large bubbles.

• **Seedy Glass** - transparent glass with small air bubbles, manufactured in various colors. The clear is often used for background.

• **Waterglass** - high gloss with a rippled surface resembling water. Also available in iridescent, clear, and color. An excellent choice for water scenes as well as all types of art objects.

• **Wispy Glass** - thin, wispy trails of white in cathedral or clear glass.

• **Found objects** - whole or broken glass dishes, bottles, lenses, semi-precious stones,

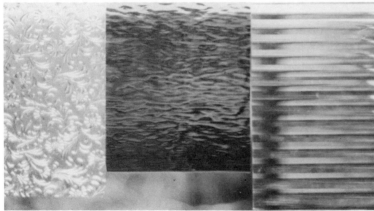

Reamy Glass,
Waterglass,
and
Ribbed Glass.

broken lead crystal glasses can be incorporated into windows or other art objects.

• **Hand-blown Rondels, faceted jewels, pressed glass pieces, globs, gems** - can be incorporated into various glass projects.

Chapter Eleven

SELECTING GLASS

Which comes first, the chicken or the egg?

"...we weave with colors all our own."

Raphael

There are many factors to consider when selecting your glass patterns and colors. The source of light, colors, textures, and styles already in the environment, the kind of color schemes you enjoy, the mood you want to evoke--all have an influence on your choices. If your art glass is for resale, select current color combinations. Visit furniture stores to see what colors and styles are currently in vogue so that your work will appeal to buyers. Before you choose colors, observe the texture and color of the walls, drapes, or other furnishings which will be near your finished piece. Decide what kind of effect is desired and which hues will convey that effect. Make sure that the color schemes are eye-catching, style-conscious, and appropriate for the viewer, not overused or outdated.

Some glass artists have a tendency to rely only on glass color to make the statement. The color alone will not carry the art without a balanced composition or interesting design. The overall combination of design, color, and texture are the unified components that make an artist's statement.

Should you draw or select the pattern first or buy the glass first? Since there is a myriad of intriguing glass from which to choose, shopping for

materials can become an exciting adventure. Visiting your glass dealer will give you ideas about color combinations that you might not otherwise visualize.

Each glass has its own character, even flaws, which can inspire you or suggest images. While selecting glass, you might see an idea in the design of the glass or a color variation which will suggest a theme that can be developed into a finished piece. Buy some of these unique pieces for your special stock to use in future projects. Mark the interesting areas in the glass with chalk, and make a note of the design that you visualize.

With pattern in hand, you can make color selections to complement your drawing. Try to work with subject matter and glass that you are enthusiastic about. You will have better results, and the whole working experience will be much more satisfying. As you look at the sheets, take your time, feel the texture. Take the glass sheets to the sunlight; study them in various light situations. If possible, take them to the area where they will be used.

The chosen one

A common error is to choose too many hues. Two or three colors usually work best. Five colors are too many. Make sure there is only one dominant color; this one color will set the tone for the entire color scheme. The other colors should be less striking in either saturation or value. Be careful of vivid colors because they can be irritating when used too freely. Since bright colors come forward, use them sparingly as accent colors, never in the background.

As a general rule, choose the color for the largest area first, then the color for the next-largest area. Varying the shades in a scheme is just as important as varying the colors themselves. Your color scheme may look lifeless if you contrast only the hues; your finished piece will look more three-dimensional and bolder if light colors are contrasted with dark ones. A common ground should be found between your colors; those chosen

Line and Color Magic for Glass Design

should be compatible or similar in some way. Using similar hues or different shades of the same hue will promote color harmony. Instead of using green and blue together, choose green-blue and blue-green.

Before choosing a final color scheme, experiment to see if your design can be improved by changing the position of the colors. Make photocopies of your original small design, and color these with markers or colored pencils. Compare the results to see if the changes create the mood, special effect, or style you want to achieve.

It is a wise idea to purchase more than enough glass to complete your design to allow for a possible cutting mistake. If you run out of a particular color while working, it may be impossible to duplicate since batches of glass can vary slightly in hue, shading, texture, or density.

Light exposure

The amount of light reaching or flowing through the finished art piece or lamp will affect the density and colors of the glass you choose. Therefore, observe your selected glass both during the day and at night if possible.

Due to the refraction of constantly changing light during the day and the seasons of the year, the dominant form or color can shift. The intensity of the sun decreases in the fall and winter and appears lower in the sky, reaching areas untouched in spring and summer.

• **Northern Exposure:**

receives the most even amount of daily light throughout the year;

• **Southern Exposure:**

has more variations of light level.

• **Eastern Exposure:**

will receive glittering morning sunlight with gradual fading as the morning proceeds.

• **Western Exposure:**

receives light from the languid afternoon sun and the shimmering, vibrant sunset. Colors lose strength and luminosity as evening falls, fading into obscure forms of gray.

• A shady room might welcome a touch of warm colors in a glass creation; a bright sunny room might need a cool color scheme to counteract glaring sun.

• If you have a large window or several windows in a room, you can afford to use darker colors, whereas if you have only one or two small windows, you can use clear textured glass or very light shaded hues.

• An area's climate also plays a role in color choice. A warm, sunny environment like Florida seems to call for a color scheme which is powerful, vibrant, and dazzling. A cooler environment receiving less sun, a Scandinavian country for example, seems to require more subtle, tranquil color harmonies.

The marriage of transparent and opalescent glass is a happy combination that bears exploration. Because of their contrast of light diffusion, they work well together-- especially in a lamp. In a window through which daylight is streaming, the opalescents will appear darker than the transparents; whereas when light diminishes at dusk, the transparent colors become less vibrant and the opalescents will appear lighter. If you have an undesirable view, the use of opalescent glass and heavily textured glass can obscure the view and "protect you from the environment."

Textures

Contrast of textures can add areas of interest, create depth, express a particular mood, and contribute rhythm through repetitive pattern. Although less important than design and color, textures should be chosen carefully as they can enhance and enrich your piece. Tactile surfaces can be rough or smooth, soft or hard, shiny or dull, fine or coarse. Smooth glass is less demanding of the viewer. Rough textures can overshadow form and color.

Textures can become the dominant attraction of a piece and must be used discriminately. They attract attention and can be very stimulating. Large textures advance toward the viewer while smaller ones retreat. Keep in mind that the eye needs rest areas in a design. Areas with little or no detail are important in coaxing the viewer's eye to move around the panel.

Textured glass was used to denote the drapes, wallpaper, blankets, and shade in this panel.

As discussed in the chapter on Line and Design, one of the elements of good design is unity and repetition. To retain consistency, repeat a texture at least two or three times. Combining too many different textures in one project results in confusion.

• Do not place bold textures on the outer edges of a panel as the eye will have a tendency to focus on them.

• Textured glass can be employed to denote objects such as floral wallpaper, heavily draped curtains, the bark of trees, the petals of flowers, foliage, water, etc.

• If you are combining stained glass with sandblasted art, select glass textures that complement the etched textures.

• Three-dimensional decorative soldered seams and ornaments have texture that should be considered and coordinated with the type of glass textures used.

"If the science of color harmony is knowing which colors to use, the art is knowing what order to put the colors in, and what proportions of each."

Hideaki Chijiiwa

Doodles and Data

Line and Color Magic for Glass Design

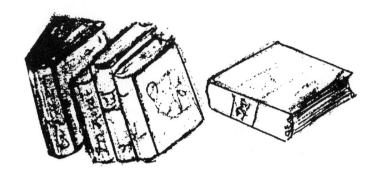

BIBLIOGRAPHY

Batt, Miles G., *The Complete Guide to Creative Watercolor*, Fort Lauderdale, Florida: Creative Art Publications, 1988.

Birren, Faber, *Creative Color*, West Chester, Pennsylvania: Schiffer Publishing Ltd., 1987.

Canady, John, *Metropolitan Seminars in Art*, New York: The Metropolitan Museum of Art, 1958.

Carini, Edward, *Take Another Look*, Englewood Cliffs, New Jersey: Prentice-Hall, Inc., 1970.

Chijiiwa, Hideaki, *Color Harmony: A Guide to Creative Color Combinations*, Rockport, Massachusetts: Rockport Publishers, 1987.

Ching, Francis D. K., *Drawing: A Creative Process*, New York: Van Nostrand Reinhold, 1990.

Color Compass, Cranbury, New Jersey: M. Grumbacher, Inc., 1972.

deFiore, Gaspare, *Drawing with Color and Imagination*, New York: Watson-Guptill Publications, 1985.

De Grandis, Luigina, *Theory and Use of Color*, New York: Harry N. Abrams, Inc., 1986.

de Sausmurez, Maurice, *Basic Design: The Dynamics of Visual Form*, New York: Reinhold Publishing Corp., 1964.

Dondis, Donis A., *A Primer of Visual Literacy*, Cambridge, Massachusetts: The Massachusetts Institute of Technology, 1974.

Edwards, Betty, *Drawing on the Right Side of the Brain*, Los Angeles: J. P. Tarcher, Inc., 1979.

Fabri, Ralph, *Color: A Complete Guide for Artists*, New York: Watson-Guptill Publications, 1967.

Gawain, Shakti, *Creative Visualization*, San Rafael, California: New World Library, 1978.

Guptill, Arthur L., *Color Manual for Artists*, New York: Van Nostrand Reinhold Company, 1980.

Kazanjian & Rosey, *How to Design for Stained Glass*, Hermosa Beach, California: Kazanjian & Rosenthal, 1977.

Menten, Theodore, *The Art Deco Style in Household Objects, Architecture, Sculpture, Graphics, Jewelry*, New York: Dover Publications, Inc., 1972.

Mirow, Gregory, *A Treasury of Design for Artists and Craftsmen*, New York: Dover Publications, Inc., 1969.

Parramon, J. M., *Composition*, Tucson: H. P. Books, 1981.

Poore, Henry Rankin, *Composition in Art*, New York: Dover Publications, Inc., 1976.

Sargent, Walter, *The Enjoyment and Use of Color*, New York: Dover Publications, Inc., 1964.

Swansea, Charleen, *Mindworks*, Columbia: South Carolina ETV and Charleen Swansea, 1990.

Weiss, Rita, *The Artist's and Craftsman's Guide to Reducing, Enlarging and Transferring Designs*, New York: Dover Publications, Inc., 1983.

Wills, F. H., *Fundamentals of Layout*, New York: Dover Publications, Inc., 1971.

Wolchonok, Louis, *Design for Artists and Craftsmen*, New York: Dover Publications, Inc., 1953.

About the author

KAY BAIN WEINER was inspired to write this book by the many fine students and talented craftspersons who expressed a need for guidance regarding color and design for glass art. Kay's life has been a creative art experience, beginning as a child in art schools. She majored in fine arts in college and has continued to study art and painting throughout the years. She has worked professionally in fused and stained glass for 28 years.

For over 20 years, Kay has written about crafts and glass for numerous publications, such as "Glass Patterns Quarterly" and "Glass Art Magazine". Most recently, Kay wrote the *Solder Magic* video tape, *Solder Magic Book, Patterns and Instructions*, and Chilton Publishers' book, *Stained Glass Magic*.

For the past eight years, Kay has been a consultant for Canfield Quality Solder. She is a workshop instructor, lecturer at art centers, colleges, and adult schools, as well as a speaker, demonstrator and seminar leader at national trade shows. She presently teaches design and solder magic workshops around the country.